The Zoo Book

The Zoo Book

a child's world of animals

TEXT BY ROBERT ALLEN

PHOTOGRAPHED IN COLOR
BY PETER SAHULA

PLATT & MUNK, *Publishers*/NEW YORK

The animals in The Zoo Book *were photographed at the New York Zoological Park (Bronx Zoo), the Central Park Zoo in New York City, and at the Zoological Gardens, Regents Park, London.*

Introduction

The animals in this book are ones you will see at the zoo, but these animals don't live just in zoos. They live all over the world in the wild.

Animals in the zoo are well fed and do not face the dangers they must overcome in nature. In the zoo, they behave much the way they do in the wild. The reason they are in the zoo is so people can see them and get to know what they are like. But you must remember that the zoo is not their natural home at all.

TIGER

Tigers don't care for the sun very much. They like to lie in the shade during the day and hunt at night. If they get too warm, they find some water and go for a swim, which is a strange thing for a cat to do. Tigers live in Asia and they usually prowl around by themselves instead of staying with other tigers. Tigers are as strong as lions, and some people think they are even more ferocious. It really doesn't matter. Meeting a lion or a tiger in the jungle would be equally scary.

POLAR BEAR

Polar bears live around the North Pole where it is very cold. Their fur is so thick that when they swim in freezing water they don't feel cold. Polar bears don't like people very much, but mothers are nice to their children. If a baby polar bear is tired, its mother will carry it on her back for a while. And sometimes she will let the baby hold her tail while she swims around. Baby polar bears have a lot to be grateful for.

MONKEY

Monkeys use their arms and tails to swing in trees like an acrobat in the circus. Monkeys are more intelligent than most animals. If you try to teach a monkey tricks, he will be happy to learn them. Monkeys have hands and feet that are like a human's, and a face that almost looks human, and monkeys like to imitate the things that humans do. If a monkey sees you scratch your head, he may scratch his head too. Most people think monkeys are very funny. Most monkeys are.

ZEBRA

Zebras live in Africa and like to run on
the wide, flat plains. One animal a zebra
always watches out for is the lion.
The lion is the zebra's worst enemy.
All zebras have stripes but no two zebras
are striped exactly alike. It's hard to tell
whether a zebra is a black animal with
white stripes or a white animal
with black stripes.

LEOPARD

Leopards are mostly yellow with black spots, but sometimes they are all black. Leopards can run very fast. They can even run up the trunks of trees and leap from branch to branch. Leopards are skillful hunters and they usually catch the animals they chase. Very few animals enjoy being chased by a leopard.

LION

Male lions have a large head and a regal mane, and that is one reason why lions are called the King of Beasts. Another reason is that they are strong and fierce. Most lions live in Africa and hunt other animals, like the zebra and the antelope, for food. Lions like to be with other lions and hardly ever go around alone. Mother lions are good to their cubs and teach them everything they know about living in the wild—except how to roar. Young lions already know how to do that.

OSTRICH

Ostriches live in Africa and they are the
largest birds you can find anywhere.
Ostriches can't fly but they can run faster
than any other bird. An ostrich is supposed
to bury its head in the sand when it's
afraid. It doesn't really do this, but
sometimes it puts its head down
on the ground to listen for footsteps.
Anyone trying to sneak up on an ostrich
had better walk quietly.

BEAR

Most bears like to live near mountains.
They have large bodies and short legs and
they look clumsy. But actually they can
do a lot of things very well. They can
climb tall trees and swim fast and catch
fish with their paws. Even though they
have a heavy fur coat, they don't like
winter very much. They go to sleep as
soon as it gets cold and may not wake up
again until spring. When a bear says
goodnight in autumn, he really means it.

SQUIRREL

Squirrels are animals that plan ahead.
When it is warm they hide nuts and fruits
and seeds so they will have something
to eat when it gets cold and there isn't
much food around. Squirrels can run up a
tree and jump around in its branches with
no trouble at all. When they are jumping,
their bushy tail helps them to balance
and steer themselves. In the woods,
squirrels are very shy, but if you see one
at a zoo or in a park, it will probably
come up and beg for a nut. Squirrels save
nuts the way people save money.

CROCODILE

Crocodiles are long and thin and have a large mouth with as many as 120 teeth. Crocodiles love to sit in the hot sun, but they have such tough, bumpy skin that they never get sunburned. Crocodiles also like to swim and when they drift on the surface of a river, they look like tall, floating trees. But trees can't bite and crocodiles can.

HIPPOPOTAMUS

Hippopotamuses like to relax in a river
and they can stay underwater for a
long time. Sometimes a hippopotamus
will go underwater and walk along the
bottom for ten minutes without coming up
for air. Sometimes a baby hippo will ride
on its mother's back while the mother
is underwater. A hippopotamus weighs as
much as 35 men, but it can run on land
faster than a man. Aren't you surprised
that a hippopotamus is so talented?

SEAL

Seals have a smooth body and webbed
flippers that help them to swim fast.
Seals can stay underwater for 15 minutes
and after a swim like that they like to
flop on a rock and enjoy the sun. Seals are
gentle and intelligent and can be taught
tricks, which is why you might see a seal
balancing a ball on its nose. Seals like
to eat fish. The best way to let a seal
know you like it is to hand it a fish.

PENGUIN

Penguins look as if they are wearing evening clothes, which is funny because they live around the South Pole where there is no place to go at night. Penguins can't fly but they can swim very fast. When they go for a swim, they leap out of the water and turn in the air like a bird flying. Penguins are very fond of other penguins and sometimes 50,000 of them live together. Penguins are plump and have short legs and waddle when they walk. Penguins sound as if someone made them up, but they are real.

GIRAFFE

Giraffes are the tallest animals in the world. They have long legs and long necks and even a long tongue—longer than your arm. Giraffes eat the leaves from tall trees. Three men standing on one another's shoulders sometimes can't reach as high as a giraffe's head. Giraffes are very shy and if anything bothers them, they gallop off at a very fast rate. When it comes to trouble, a giraffe will never stick its neck out.

RHINOCEROS

Rhinoceroses aren't very smart and they have a bad temper besides. Rhinoceroses can't see very well and spend most of the time sleeping or eating. Rhinoceroses have a very thick skin, short fat legs and a bumpy horn on their nose. Rhinoceroses aren't very handsome. Some people think that only a mother rhinoceros can love a baby rhinoceros. Maybe that is true.

GORILLA

Gorillas live in the forests of Africa and they are the largest kind of ape. Gorillas are extremely strong. They look as if they hate everyone except other gorillas, but actually they hardly ever attack other animals. They eat vegetables and fruits and live quietly in small families. Gorillas resemble humans and they can stand up the way a man does, but most of the time they walk on all fours, using their arms and their legs. A gorilla knows very well that it is a gorilla.

PARROT

Parrots have large heads and hooked beaks.
They live in a warm climate and look
like someone has spilled bright-colored
paint on their feathers. Parrots like
company and they can be taught to speak
the way humans do. Don't be surprised
if you hear a parrot say: "Good morning"
or "Give me a banana split with
whipped cream, please."

BISON

Bison have shaggy manes, sharply-curved
horns and a wispy beard. Once there were
lots of bison in America, but when
Americans settled the western United
States, they killed many of these animals
for food and for their hides. There are
very few bison left, and it is against
the law to kill one now. Bison eat grass,
leaves, twigs and bark. The way
they have been treated, it's a wonder
they don't eat people.

ANTELOPE

Antelopes are swift and graceful. They live
in Africa and Asia and usually travel
around in large groups. There are many
different kinds of antelopes. Some are
as small as a rabbit, others are larger
than a lion. Antelopes can run faster than
most animals, and they often do. A crowd
of antelopes speeding across the grass is
gone before you know it.

ELEPHANT

Some people think an elephant's trunk is the most interesting part of an elephant, and they may be right. With its trunk, an elephant can put food in its mouth, give itself a shower and pull a tree out of the ground. Elephants are the biggest animals that live on land. Most of them are quite smart and have good memories, but sometimes they forget things, just as people do. One thing an elephant never forgets is that it likes peanuts.

OWL

Most owls live deep in the woods. They
have large heads and staring eyes and they
look a lot smarter than they really are.
They fly around at night, so silently that
it's hard to hear them coming, except
when they make a noise that sounds like
"whoo, whoo, whoo." Even though owls
go about their business after the sun goes
down, they see very well. An owl never
stubs its toe on a tree in the dark.

CAMEL

Camels with one hump live in the desert and those with two humps live in snowy places. Both kinds of camels can go for days without food and water and can travel long distances carrying heavy loads. They have soft, padded feet which don't sink very far into sand or snow, and their eyes are protected by a double set of eyelashes. Camels store fat inside a hump and live on this fat when there is no food to eat. The size of the hump shows how much fat the camel has left. A camel with a very small hump should be given a meal right away.

KANGAROO

Kangaroos come from Australia and one
thing they do well is jump. If they get
tired, they stand up to rest on their
tail. Baby kangaroos never have to
worry about getting where they want to go.
They ride in a little pouch in their
mother's stomach. Sometimes they come
out to play, but when they feel sleepy,
they go right back inside. A kangaroo's
pouch is probably the nicest baby carriage
ever made.

PELICAN

A pelican is the only bird that has a
traveling picnic basket. Its basket is
a pouch in the pelican's bill. When a
pelican dives down into the water and
catches a fish in its bill, it doesn't have to
swallow the fish right away. It can hold
the fish in its pouch for a while.
Very few fish ever get out of a pelican's
pouch alive.

GOAT

Goats are good at climbing and they go up the side of a mountain as easily as people climb stairs, taking long leaps from one ledge to the next. Goats are useful animals. They give milk and their wool is made into cloth. They live all over the world, sometimes in the wild, sometimes on a farm or a ranch. Male goats have horns and usually a beard. Sometimes a goat will swallow strange things, like paper, ribbons or a rubber ball. Never leave anything you like near a hungry goat.

TURTLE

A turtle's shell is like a suit of armor.
When a turtle puts its feet and head
inside, the shell becomes a roof—and it
never leaks. The turtle is protected from
the weather and from its enemies, too.
Maybe that's why some turtles live
to be 175, older than any other animal
in the world. Or maybe they live so long
because they don't tire themselves out
by running too fast.